ENJOY!

Love,

Willie

Signs, Signals and Clues

The Joy of Tracking Your Life
in Partnership with Spirit

WILLIE CARTER

BALBOA.
PRESS
A DIVISION OF HAY HOUSE

Balboa Press books may be ordered through booksellers or by contacting:
Balboa Press
A Division of Hay House
1663 Liberty Drive
Bloomington, IN 47403
www.balboapress.com
1-(877) 407-4847

Printed in the United States of America

ISBN: 978-1-4525-6543-9 (sc)
ISBN: 978-1-4525-6545-3 (hc)
ISBN: 978-1-4525-6544-6 (e)

Library of Congress Control Number: 2012923531

Balboa Press rev. date: 2/01/2013

For

Barry

Michelle

Kris

Contents

Acknowledgments

I would like to thank my husband, Barry, from the bottom of my heart, for his continual love and support of my ideas, adventures and explorations of anything and everything to do with spirit, the universe and the on-going creation of my experiences on this planet. You are my rock!

Two of the greatest joys of my life are my children. They have kept me honest and authentic on my journey here and with the writing of Signs, Signals and Clues. I so admire and am inspired by their commitment to their own creative journey, Michelle as a singer-songwriter and Kris as a visual artist. Thank you, Kris, for the wonderful drawings that you provided for Signs, Signals and Clues and Michelle, for the beautiful song you wrote in honor of this book.

Many thanks to my focus group: Michelle Carter, Ingrid Moerman, Arlene Soloman, and Heather White. Your combined experience, wisdom and practical, loving feedback kept me focused on the task at hand, especially at times when I felt like giving up.

To my twin cousin, Maion Davidson (our Moms were twins, married best friends on the same day and we were born on the same day, nine months later!): Many thanks for your generosity in allowing me to share a couple of your stories and for always being there for me.

To my sister, Ingrid: Many thanks for your continued love and inspiring support as I moved through this project and for allowing me to share your story.

My heartfelt thanks to Steve MacDonald at the University of Santa Monica for all the practical support and guidance he provided as I was completing this project. His patience, expertise and wisdom as a writer helped me to appreciate and share what I had to offer.

To Drs. Ron and Mary Hulnick: Thank you for providing such a rich environment for giving birth to this project.

To my project team: Giselle Paquet, Melanie Real and Harpreet Vitale: Thank you for listening to the stories of my trials and tribulations on the journey of writing this book, for not buying into the stories and for your encouragement in keeping me on task with the completion of this book.

To the staff at Balboa Press, particularly Heather Perry, Brandon G., Andrea Geasey and Matthew Haynes: Many thanks for your patience and support in answering my many questions and helping to move my book forward.

To all the people I have had the privilege of working with: for opening up your hearts and being willing to be vulnerable with me while we explored your souls` journey. I have learned so much from each of you.

And last but not least to my own guides, Spirit, the universe. It`s so much more fun not doing this journey alone. Thank you for the signs, signals and clues you send me on a daily basis and for inspiring me to create this book.

Introduction

Why did I want to write this book? I wanted you to feel in charge of your life, to realize that you have options—that you have the power to create the life that you designed before coming here. I want you to have fun looking for and using the clues. I want you to know that there's a much easier way to live life.

Over the past twenty-five years, I've had the privilege of working with many people from all walks of life through my various roles at a crisis and counseling center, in a victim services program, in the justice system, and as a life and career coach. I have met amazing people who have had very difficult lives, and I've learned so much from each of them. The common thread that I noticed running through the human condition was a high level of self-abuse. I believe this is the real source of most suffering in the world. The enemy is within.

On October 6, 2009, in the middle of the night sometime, I woke up with the title *Signs, Signals, and Clues* in my head.

Actually, it started off with just the word *signs,* and then it expanded into the rest. I was so excited; not a crazy excitement but a grounded, very satisfied excitement. *Yes! This is what I'm meant to write about. It totally fits. This is my passion, my interest—always has been.*

Then when I got up in the morning, I thought, *Oh, there are at least a million people who know more about signs than I do.* Then I thought, *Wait a minute—but no one with my exact experience and perspective.*

I first became interested in clues as a young girl when I spent time out in nature. I took books out of the library to teach me how to track animals, learn about rocks, and learn about the cycles of nature in the trees, plants, and flowers. I loved looking at and reading clouds. I just knew that Spirit had a purpose for everything—that nothing was wasted. I found that fascinating. And as I got older, I became very interested in mysteries. I became fixated on my favorite detective shows and detective novels. At the same time, I was just as interested in science, religion, the mysteries of life, the universe, … There was no end to the fascinating things that could be studied.

To this day, I still *love* looking for clues. It's my passion—my hobby. Solving puzzles, Sudoku, codes, symbols, figuring things out all help me to hone and master my skills in noticing the clues.

You are the **author** and **author**-ity of your own life. My biggest wish for you is that, through this book, you will be inspired to create a new story for yourself. There are over seven billion of us on the planet now who are here to experience being creators.

We are **flow**-ers of energy, and how we use and direct this energy is our choice. And we don't have to do it alone. There are guides awaiting our requests for help in managing this energy. Spirit is experiencing and expressing itself through you.

I intend to have this book be a joyful journey in tracking your life in partnership with Spirit. The gift you bring to the world, as your unique self, is your **perspective**. This is your treasure chest of gold. How you operate, how you are in this world, what you love, and how you love matters.

Your only job is to show up, wonder about, and be curious about your own life. Your own life is fascinating. It's an adventure. Enjoy your adventure!

Chapter 1

It's All about You

You designed this journey on planet Earth before you were born, and you left yourself a map and a guidance system for what you wanted to experience in this lifetime. This map is written in your dreams and your desires. How come you're interested in this and not that? This map is written in the patterns of your family experience, your body, and your name. Your guidance system is encoded in your feelings, thoughts, and beliefs. Just like a rocket shooting into space, there will be different periods in your life where you will be boosted out of your comfort zone and propelled forward into another level of the stratosphere according to your life design.

You are guided moment to moment to live the life that you have designed for yourself, and you will know when you are on track by your noticings, that is, by what you notice, by what grabs your attention. Why are you noticing this and not that? Your only job is to wonder about and be curious about your own life which will then lead you to take inspired action.

You have chosen to come to planet Earth to play with energy, to manage energy, and to create with this energy. What is this energy? It's universal energy—the unformed energy of the universe that connects all of us and everything in the universe. And it finds expression through you. You are a creator in training, and you are in training with every other person on the planet. Wow! With each breath that you inhale you are connecting to the flow of universal energy, and with each exhale, you are connecting with the earth. You are the conduit between heaven and earth, expressing your life stream of energy in your own unique way.

With each breath, you are also connecting with the universal field of consciousness. Thoughts from this field are constantly passing through you. Through your focus and attention, you manage the flow of this energy. Your thoughts are what create and tell the story of your life. Your feelings are a physical response to these thoughts that let you know whether you are on track with the story that you are creating. They are your guidance system—your GPS—and they let you know what direction to take next. Each of you, when you were born, set an intention to experience a variety of circumstances in your life that would facilitate the learning and expansion you want to accomplish during this lifetime. You designed your own itinerary.

Working in partnership with Spirit, your job is to get clear about and ask for what you want. Your longings and desires are clues about what wants to be born through you. What wants to be expressed through you? What is it that you want to experience—today, tomorrow, next year? Your guides and higher self are always sending you signs, signals, and clues based on your intentions. Because of free will, they can't interfere by telling you what to do. They can't make decisions for you. (Darn!) But once you ask for help, they can then send you signs, signals, and clues to guide you along in making your decisions and expressing your creations.

Just like the world of advertising and marketing gets your attention through **signs** (billboards, logos, slogans, images), **signals** (flashing lights, "buy now" signs), and **clues**, the universe does the same. Just as the language of dreams is very unique and personal to the dreamer, so the language of Spirit is unique and personal to you and your guides. Your job is to be aware of what they're sending you. This means getting to know the language of Spirit—**your** Spirit.

It's like going to detective school. How do you learn to become a detective? How do you learn to become a tracker? And what is it that you are tracking? You are tracking your energy.

Your **perspective** is your gift to the world. How you see things is your own unique contribution. Here is where your role as the witness to your own life comes in. If you were to just observe your life and yourself in your life, you would find all of it quite fascinating. And out of that fascination and wonderment, you would receive answers—answers that you might never have thought of or answers that are, in fact, so simple that you have completely missed the obvious.

I now invite you to go on this journey with me, and explore your world through your eyes. So, let's get started!

Ask

Notice

Act

Ask for What You Want

CHAPTER 2

Ask for What You Want

Y OUR JOB, AS A CO-CREATOR with Spirit, is to ask for what you want. Asking gets the ball rolling. One of the ways that you manage your energy—the piece of the pie of universal energy that is expressed through you—is by asking for what you want. Until you ask for what you want, Spirit can't step in. Spirit can't interfere. It's a universal law—no one can interrupt your free will. Asking for signs gives you a direct line to the universe. What is your **quest**? What do you want an answer to? What is it that you want to ask for? You can ask for help with anything.

The first thing to do is to give yourself permission to ask. Have a little chat with yourself. What is it that you really, really want? Imagine it. Dream about it. Pretend you already have it in your life. How does it feel? There are basically two feelings: either you feel good or you don't. If something feels good, great!

You can ask to be shown your next steps in moving toward it. If it doesn't feel good, then that is information for you. Pay attention. Is this really your dream or someone else's?

What is your purpose in asking for a sign? Here are some possibilities for what you might want to receive answers to:

* The location of lost and found items
* Questions about relationships
* Help with homework, exams, or deadlines
* Questions about buying gifts, a house, or a car
* Career/job issues
* Health concerns
* Finances/money challenges
* Education
* Fun/travel/entertainment

Something wants to be born through you. You know this, because you feel an attraction—a desire—to experience this something. It may be a thing, an activity, a quality, or meeting a certain person. Maybe part of this life's journey is that you want to experience what it feels like to be a mom, become a mountain climber, start a business, or learn a new language. Why is it that you are interested in this and not that?

Pay attention to this desire that you feel. It has a message for you. Notice what you notice. What catches your attention? Notice what you see, hear, smell, or feel. Notice what you have a reaction to. (See Chapter 3 for more details.) Then take the next step, and see how that feels. If you don't know what you want, you can ask for signs about that, too.

Asking the Right Question

I LOVE ASKING QUESTIONS. QUESTIONS OPEN up your world to possibilities. The answers are all around us, but until we ask the right question, we aren't able to see the answer. Asking the right question is the key that opens up the portal to the stream of universal consciousness that delivers the answers to us and helps us to recognize the answer.

To get the right answer, it's important to ask the right **quest**-ion. Asking the right question opens the portal to **your** treasure chest of answers. You know if a question is useful and benevolent based on your reaction to it. You can tell if you're asking the right question by how you feel. When you ask the right question—that is, the question that fits the answer to what you're looking for—you may feel:

* Uplifted
* Joyful
* Excited
* Inspired
* Like something has landed
* Butterflies in your belly
* Relieved
* Relaxed
* Peaceful
* Expanded

Some examples of the right question may include:

* What do I want?

* What do I want to experience?

* How do I want to feel?

* What makes me feel good?

* What inspires me?

* What makes me smile?

* What do I love doing?

* What can I do for fun?

* What is important to me?

* What message is there in this situation/challenge/problem/issue facing me?

* What is trying to get my attention?

* What is it about this that matters to me?

* What wants to be born?

* What wants to be expressed through me?

* What are my next steps?

* What direction do I take?

Asking the Wrong Question

*H*OW CAN YOU TELL WHEN you're asking the wrong question? When you ask the wrong question, it doesn't feel good. You may notice that:

* It's like a tape that plays over and over in your mind, and it never has an answer.
* It has an element of self-abuse, self-neglect, and self-denial about it.
* You get answers from others that don't feel right.
* It leads to more questions.
* It feels like an interrogation.
* It feels confusing.
* It feels like work.
* It feels heavy.
* You feel imprisoned.
* You feel like a victim.
* It feels like a "should."
* It has an element of blame or self-blame.
* It makes you want to rebel (the inner civil war between the shoulds and the shouldn'ts).

Some examples of asking the wrong question may include:

* How am I ever going to get out of this mess?

* How did I ever let myself get into this mess?

* Why won't they listen to me?

* Why do I procrastinate?

* Why don't I feel good?

* Why can't I quit?

* What am I doing wrong?

* Why am I not more organized?

* What's the matter with me?

* Why can't I seem to …?

* Why am I such a screw-up?

* What's wrong with me/you/them?

Even the question you're asking is a clue as to whether you're on track or not. When you ask the right question, you'll feel an energy shift. You'll feel lighter. The wrong question feels heavy. Your reaction will tell you whether you've asked the right question or not. If you ask the wrong question, it will keep you stuck in your old story.

In my second year of university, one of my roommates noticed that wherever she went, there was a horrible smell. My other roommates and I couldn't smell it. She obviously had a much better developed sense of smell than we did. What were we missing? If we couldn't smell this, then how could we be sure that we ourselves weren't the ones creating the odor? Was that why some people were avoiding me? It turned out that my roommate had a serious infection in her nose that created an awful smell that followed her everywhere. We were asking the wrong questions.

How to Ask the Right Question

* Be heartfelt.

* Be curious; this creates openness to the possibilities.

* Be clear. Ask, *Why is this important to me? Why am I asking this question? Is it because I want an answer or because someone else does (e.g., family, friends, society, or culture)?*

* What is **your** quest?

* Whatever you ask for, always include as part of your asking the words, *for the highest good of all concerned.*

* Expect and trust that you will get an answer to your question. Recognize that the answer may not come in the package or the way that you expect.

* Once you've asked the question, let it go.

* Express appreciation when you receive the answer.

How to Ask the Wrong Question

* Make assumptions.

* Be judgmental.

* Try to control and manipulate the question by being realistic.

* Micro-manage the universe by telling it how your desire should be delivered.

* Take things personally.

* Blame others or yourself.

* Have an agenda; be attached to the outcome.

Micro-managing the universe

Letting Go

NOTICE YOUR REACTION TO THIS moment. Your job is to notice where you're being guided based on your question. What do you want to keep? What do you want to let go of? You know when you're going through a shift when you finally say to yourself, *I just can't do this anymore; I just can't live this way anymore.* You have just made a declaration for change.

What is it that you just can't do anymore? In this moment, identify what it is that you're letting go of. Be specific. Ask for help in letting go, and/or ask for help in identifying what you're moving toward. If you're not clear about where you're going, ask for clues about that. If you're unclear about what direction to take, ask for clues to give you clarity.

Clearly define the result you want. Imagine that it is done. Have fun dreaming about it. Then say thank you to complete this cycle. Now let it go. Don't give it another thought; return to this present moment, and take care of what's in front of you.

Trust

*A*SKING QUESTIONS HELPS YOU TO clarify and identify what you're looking for. Underlying all of this is the ability to trust. Trust is a muscle you build through practice. Start small. Many people have started by asking for parking spaces. As they get in the habit of asking for and receiving parking spaces, they begin to trust that their parking spaces are available when they want them, wherever they are. Eventually, this becomes their norm. They come to believe that they will always find their parking spaces easily and effortlessly.

Imagine even bigger things becoming part of your norm. When you ask for help, expect to receive guidance. As you develop the habit of noticing, paying attention, and listening, your trust in these messages will increase. It's a lack of trust that has gotten you into trouble in the past when you've second-guessed your first inklings.

Setting an Intention

*B*Y ASKING A QUESTION OR making a request, you set an intention. You have given a direction and focus to the energy that is streaming through you. This is what plugs you into your direction, destination, and goals. Where do you intend for your energy to go? What is it that you want to create? As a co-creator with the universe, your job is to be grounded. (Remember, you're the connector between the spirit world and the earth). Your job is to plug in. What do you intend your experience to be for this day? For this morning? For this moment?

If you are plugged into worrying, complaining, fretting, judging, assuming, blaming, or chastising (whether yourself or others), then you are recycling old, stagnant energy. It's like doing today's dishes in yesterday's water and expecting amazing results! You are recycling the same old intentions. And guess what? You continue to get more of the same. Surprise!

You are already in the habit of setting intentions. When you get in your car, most of the time, you have a clear intention for your destination. When you sit down to eat, you have a clear intention to appease your hunger. You can enrich these experiences by setting a clear intention to arrive safely and punctually at your destination while having a peaceful, fun drive along the way. You can enrich your eating experience by intending to find a great place to eat where you can sit outside in the sun and be taken care of by an attentive server while you enjoy the perfect food for your body at that time.

Intention can only happen in this moment. Focus on what you want. What is your intention? You can set an intention to notice the clues for your goals easily and effectively and for the highest good of all concerned. Set your intention at the beginning of the day to notice the signs, signals, and clues that will answer your questions for the day.

What you focus on dictates where you are plugged in. Being plugged in connects the flow of your energy to create what you are focused on. For example, today I intend to explore options for a new apartment. I intend to notice the clues easily and effectively so that this apartment can be manifested in a way that is for the highest good of all concerned.

If I don't know what I want in a new apartment, then I might ask for clues that will help me to identify what I want. If I don't know the best area to live in, then I might ask for clues about that. Or I might ask for clues about the best landlord and the best budget for me. I might ask, *What are my next steps?*

One year, my husband's birthday was fast approaching, and I didn't have a clue what to get him. Buying a gift may not seem like a big deal or something even worth asking Spirit about, but I get really stressed out and paralyzed by my indecision. So I called in my team for help. I asked for guidance and inspiration. An idea popped into my mind—to buy my husband a set of binoculars. I went shopping at one store that carried six different types of binoculars. I was overwhelmed by choices. I didn't know what I was looking for or what questions to ask, so I went home and asked for more guidance.

Two days before his birthday, I still didn't know what to get. However, I continued to notice what I noticed. I got the urge to call a friend who I hadn't seen in a while and asked her if she wanted to meet. We decided to go for a walk at a beautiful park alongside a river. As we were walking, she told me about her recent birthday and how she had received two sets of binoculars for her birthday. Imagine that! What were the chances?

It turned out that she knew quite a bit about binoculars. After telling her about my gift idea for my husband and my paralysis in moving forward with this idea, she asked me several pertinent questions. All of a sudden, she suggested that we go to the store, which just `happened` to be about a two-minute walk from where we were. Within twenty minutes, I had bought the perfect set of binoculars for my husband's birthday.

It was so easy—once I let go. What I had to do to get there was:

* Get clear on what the end result was—a gift for my husband that he would love and that I would enjoy giving.

* Ask for help in getting those binoculars for him, since I didn't know where to start.

* Let go, and expect to receive an answer.

* Follow any promptings I had. (Notice that the prompting I had was not related to buying binoculars.)

We don't know how our signals, clues, and signs will show up. If you were looking for binoculars, you may have been prompted to turn on the TV at some point and 'happened' to land on a channel talking about binoculars, or you may have had the urge to go surfing on the web.

Remember, I said you could ask for help with anything. Asking doesn't always come in the form of a question. Sometimes there are no words but instead a request from the heart. My cousin, Maion, had been given a beautiful pair of pearl earrings by her mother. Maion really enjoyed wearing these earrings and often wore them to work. One day, after coming home from work, she realized that one of her earrings was missing. She was very disappointed. The next day, she looked around her office and asked her coworkers if anyone had found her earring. No one had.

About two weeks later, Maion was walking through the snow to work. It was the middle of winter, and it had been snowing heavily for the previous ten days. Snow plows had been out day after day, and the snow was now hard-packed.

As she was thoroughly enjoying her walk to work in the snow, her lost earring came to mind. She thought, *Too bad I never found my earring. It's like finding a needle in a haystack.* With her very next step, she looked down, and there it was—the white pearl earring! It had appeared like magic, packed in the snowy sidewalk. It was the very same color as the snow! Maion was shaking when she got to work. She couldn't believe what had happened.

As you can see, nothing is too small to ask for help from Spirit. The reason Maion was able to find her earring is that she had a genuine, heartfelt desire to find it, and she was totally absorbed and relaxed as she enjoyed her walk to work. This made it easy for the messages to come through.

Notice What You Notice

CHAPTER 3

Notice What You Notice

WHAT IS YOUR WAY OF receiving information? Are you a person who primarily sees things? Or are you more likely to notice sounds, such as hearing music or the words in a song? Or are you a person who feels things, such as shivers or breezes, or do you feel antsy? I am not a music person. I am not likely to notice the words in a song, because I usually can't decipher the words. I am much more likely to see something out of the ordinary.

When the phone rings, we all know that someone on the other end of the phone is trying to reach us. That person could also have tried to reach us through e-mail, text messaging, regular post, etc. But in this case, the sender decided that a phone call would be the quickest mode of communication. Spirit does the same thing. Spirit always uses the most efficient means to get your attention.

When you answer the phone, you have a choice as to whether or not to pick up the phone. Maybe you're in another room, and you don't hear the phone. Maybe the TV is too loud. Maybe you're working on a project or visiting with someone and don't want to be disturbed.

In the first case, there is too much other stimulation going on, so you miss the signal. In the other case, you notice the signal, but you make a conscious decision to ignore it. Maybe you want or need more information, so you look to see who's calling. The number is an **external sign**. Do you recognize it? Yes? No? Either way, you get a gut feeling about whether or not to answer the phone (an **internal sign**). A feeling will either feel good or bad. If it's good, you take the call; if it's not good, you don't take the call. Or you let logic take over. Logic leads you to ask, *Should I or shouldn't I?*—either/or, this or that will happen.

A ringing phone is a fairly long signal. A signal from the universe is usually short and sweet. The reaction times are much shorter or appear negligible, but the results are the same. The sender wants to get the attention of the receiver. The receiver responds to the signal, ignores it or totally misses it.

So how do you insure that you are receiving messages? By operating from a place of wonderment, *I wonder why I just noticed that.* Then start collecting clues by putting yourself in the position of being a witness to your life. *Isn't my reaction to that interesting? I wonder what that's all about. What is this clue about? What question is it answering? What has been on my mind lately? What direction is it sending me in?* Stay curious!

Often, in hindsight, you'll notice the multitude of clues that came your way. You don't need to know why you've noticed something. You just need to be aware of, acknowledge, and register the fact that you've had a reaction to or curiosity about this noticing. Eventually, the dots connect, and you'll have your answer.

Noticing What You Notice

Get in the habit of noticing—not as a chore but as an adventure. There are many ways to practice noticing.

Physically

* Notice your body.
* Feel your bum in the chair, your feet on the floor, and your clothes against your skin.
* When you eat, feel the food in your mouth, the warmth or cold of the food, and the texture of the food.
* Notice the sounds you hear as you walk down the street.
* Notice what you smell as you walk down the street.

Pick one and practice. Have fun with it. See how much you can notice.

MENTALLY

* Notice what's going on in your mind.
* What is your normal stream of thinking? Ninety-five percent of the thoughts we think are the same as the thoughts we had the day before.
* Notice when something different pops into your mind.

EMOTIONALLY

* Notice what you're feeling. The best way to notice what you're feeling is to notice what's happening in your body. The mind will play tricks on you, but the body never lies.
* Notice when you have a reaction to something. No matter what's going on around you, your reaction **always** provides information about you.

The purpose of these exercises is to discover your **norm**. What is **normal** for you? If you ever watch any detective or police shows, you'll notice the detectives beginning their investigations by discovering what the norm in the victim's life was. They determine a baseline for the victim's life. They ask neighbors, friends, and family what the victim's normal (standard) routine was so that they can determine what was out of the norm at the time of the victim's disappearance. They measure a person's normal way of being and compare it to anything unusual. They are looking for patterns and changes in patterns.

When I was going to university to get my science degree, I was hired as a summer student to work in the crime lab at national police headquarters. I worked in the toxicology department, where human tissue from suspicious deaths was analyzed for drug content. My job as a lab technician was to analyze all the various types of prescription drugs available on the market. This was called 'standardizing' the drugs. That way, we had a blueprint of what each drug looked like. This gave us a foundation to work from when analyzing tissue. The blueprint of the tissue would be compared to the blueprint of the standardized drugs, and this helped to determine what types of drugs were in the tissue. This information was then used as evidence in court. Without the standards to compare to, it would have been much more difficult to figure out what was in the tissue.

So, take a look at your own life. What are your standards? What is your **norm**? Knowing this will give you a baseline from which you can then recognize and interpret the clues you receive. For example, if an animal were to cross your path and it was out of your **norm** to see such an animal, then, based on your reaction, there may be a message there for you.

You tend to get answers when you're:

* Here/present (not time traveling)
* Curious
* Relaxed
* Non-judgmental
* Unattached to the outcome
* Grounded

What you notice is usually related to:

*   An intention you've set
*   A question you've asked
*   Your next steps based on the intention you set and question you asked

What you notice will correspond to the energy level at which you are operating. For clearer answers, raise your energy. You can raise your energy by:

*   Looking at something beautiful
*   Playing with a pet
*   Reading poetry (because of the rhythm and cadence)
*   Listening to music
*   Spending time in nature
*   Being curious

Raising Your Energy Level

Being Curious

WHAT DOES BEING CURIOUS REALLY mean? It means to come from a place of wonderment. *Isn't that interesting? I wonder what it would feel like to experience such-and-such. I wonder what message this experience has for me.* Being curious means you have left your assumptions and judgments behind. You are seeing things and people with fresh eyes—and more importantly, with a fresh heart.

What is the difference between curiosity and nosiness, you might ask? Nosiness has an agenda to it. Nosiness may be about gathering information that you can later use against someone else, to be in the know, or to outdo others in your circle. You win the round of gossip. Being curious has no charge to it. It's authentic—pure. True curiosity is what helps an inventor devise a new creation and a scientist find out how things work. True curiosity always leads to creativity.

> *The important thing is not to stop questioning. Curiosity has its own reason for existing. One cannot help but be in awe when he contemplates the mysteries of eternity, of life, of the marvelous structure of reality. It is enough if one tries merely to comprehend a little of this mystery every day. Never lose a holy curiosity. —Albert Einstein*

Noticing the clues is a matter of creating new habits. We tend to notice things when they become a problem, when in fact, the signs are there long before. So what does it take to notice clues? How do you go about developing new habits in this regard? Pick something simple to start with—something that you definitely want an answer to but that you can also detach from. Let's use the example of picking a good place to eat.

Play with this for a week or so, and see what happens. Set the intention that wherever you eat, you will have great food and great service. Ask to be guided to the best places, and then watch for the clues.

Are You a Time Traveler?

OST OF US ARE TIME travelers. While our bodies keep us anchored in the here and now, our minds take us to all kinds of places in all kinds of time zones. When you're time traveling, you are not here, and you need to be here—in this moment—to see the clues.

Why do we time travel? We do so because we have not given importance to the present moment. We believe that we are supposed to be doing something other than what we are doing—something more important. But what could be more important than this moment—which, if you are paying attention, will lead you to your next steps?

Interpreting the Signs—
Connecting the Dots

*T*HE UNIVERSE IS NOT GOING to send you signs that make no sense to you or that you can't recognize. It will speak to you in your own language. In order to recognize the clues, you need to have an idea of what you're looking for so that you can connect the dots. One clue by itself doesn't give you much (or any) direction. Several clues start to create a picture for you. What's been on your mind lately? What have you been asking for? Clues don't always come in pretty packages. We usually see what we expect to see, not what's actually there. Sometimes clues are presented as a loss.

You expect to get a certain job and don't. You are devastated. It was perfect for you—almost. Three months later, the company files for bankruptcy; meanwhile, you have actually gotten something even better. How did you not see the clues? When you're attached to the outcome, you miss the clues. If you look back, you did have niggles or concerns about that particular job but you overrode those. You didn't listen.

Pay attention when you hear yourself saying: *That's okay. I don't mind. I can handle it. It's not a big deal.* This is a big red flag that you are not listening. You are tolerating and minimizing your experience, and as a result, you may miss out on important information. How do you listen to your clues? How do you know when something's a clue and when it isn't? You know it's a clue when you have a reaction to something. It either feels good or it doesn't. If it isn't a clue, you'll just feel neutral—but more than likely, you wouldn't even notice the clue.

Our feelings are codes for alerting us when we are disconnected from Spirit—when we are unplugged from Source energy. When we're unplugged, we misinterpret the codes. Your feelings let you know where your energy's at. Your feelings will let you know what it's about. Feelings like resentment and sadness will be about the past. These same feelings may also be about the future but they are based on interpretations you have made about the past that you are now using as your platform to imagine your future.

Worry is using your imagination to create the life you don't want. Consider that your bad feelings are signposts that show you you've taken a detour. Stop, and take a look at what's really going on. Check inside. What are you really feeling? Don't whitewash it or bypass it by minimizing it. (Some people call this spiritual bypass.) If you overlook your feelings, they'll be left on the side of the road, and soon you'll have a traffic jam.

Criteria for Interpreting Signs

*T*O RECOGNIZE AND INTERPRET SIGNS, you need awareness and curiosity. Set the intention that you are open to noticing and receiving signs. After that, stay present from moment to moment, and notice what you notice. Eventually, this will become second nature.

Once you notice a sign, stay curious. *I wonder what that was about. Does it make sense in light of anything going on in my life? What is my reaction to this clue?* Remember, when you notice something, something is trying to get your attention. There is always information in what you notice.

In one period of my life, I spent a whole week noticing things about **Nova Scotia**. I'd open a magazine, and there would be an ad for **Nova Scotia**. I'd be watching TV, and something would come up about **Nova Scotia**. I'd hear people talking about **Nova Scotia** next to me in a café. It seemed to be all around me. I began to wonder why. Were we going on a trip to Nova Scotia? Not that I knew of. Were we going to buy property in Nova Scotia? I didn't really have an interest, but you never know. So what was going on in my life that this might be relevant to? I couldn't connect it to anything.

About a week later, I was in Vancouver, apartment-hunting with my daughter, Michelle. After looking at two places that we didn't like at all, we were getting discouraged. As we turned a corner and started walking down another street, we noticed a vacancy sign on the front lawn of a rather ordinary, small building. At that moment, a young man came bouncing down the steps of this building and told us that this building had wonderful apartments, and people only moved out if they were buying a place elsewhere. He turned out to be a realtor.

The vacancy sign indicated that the apartment had everything I was looking for. Intrigued, I called the number and left a message. The next day, the landlord called me back and said the place had already been taken but that he had just received word that another apartment was becoming available. He didn't know when, but the tenants were moving to **NOVA SCOTIA**. I ended up having to wait five months, but it was worth it. I knew it was the right apartment because I loved it on sight, and knowing about the people moving to Nova Scotia confirmed it.

As you can see, clues don't come in a nice, little, straight line. Life is a game, and this is one of the fun parts of playing it.

Clueless

O N THE OTHER HAND, THERE have been times when I've been downright clueless. A while back, I worked in the prosecutor's office as the regional manager of a program serving victims of crime. As with many social service jobs there was too much to do, not enough staff, and not enough time. I was getting burned out. My health was being affected, so I took a leave of absence for a few weeks.

One morning early in my leave, I decided to get my hair cut in the big city four hours away. I made an appointment for 4:00 p.m. that same day, and I invited my fifteen-year-old daughter, Michelle, to go with me. About an hour into the drive, we arrived at a small town. It was lunch time, and we were hungry, so we stopped at a fast food place. This place was not a drive-in but took orders and brought your food to your car. I waited for a server. No one came. Being in a hurry, I entered the restaurant to place my order with a young woman who stood behind a small counter. She couldn't take my order but directed me to another counter, where I proceeded to give my order to the manager behind the counter. He didn't appear to have heard me. Being soft-spoken, I repeated my order.

As I did this, I noticed how inefficient the place was. First of all, no one had attended to us outside. And now I was getting horrible service inside. Everybody was so slow! No movement. Just standing around. No action. *What's the matter with this place? Typical small town. Probably couldn't get good help. If I was running this place, I'd have everyone hopping! And look at the layout! This place needs a good reorganization. Even the cash register is in a vulnerable spot. A customer could easily come along and just ... Oh my God!* The light bulb went on! No wonder no one appeared to be working. Everyone was standing around and looking at me like I had three heads.

I had just given my order to a customer—not once, but twice! Because I had come in through the back door, I had ended up on the wrong side of the counter. I still needed to eat, so I tucked my tail between my legs, went around to the right side of the counter, and stood behind the person who I had thought was the 'manager'. When I got back in the car with our lunches, I told Michelle that it was a good thing that she hadn't come in with me. On hearing the story, she immediately slid off her seat and hid under the dash board until we were out of sight.

Had I been paying attention, I might have asked myself why I thought it was necessary to go to a city four hours away for a day trip just to get a haircut. Well, I had had a very good haircut at this place about a year or two before, but the same hairdresser wasn't there anymore. There were perfectly excellent hairdressers in our town just half an hour away. That should have been my first clue that something was off.

Was I in my body? No, I was in my head, feeling very righteous about everything, making assumptions, and being just a tad judgmental. There you have it—a perfect example of being clueless. I was not present. I was not in the moment. I saw only what I expected to see. Did you notice any judgments? Right from the get go, my judgments were the glue that kept me going down that embarrassing path, because I thought I was so right and that everyone else was so wrong. Not a great recipe for seeing the clues!

Being Clueless

Another time, when I was still working long hours at the same job, I was on my way to work with my eight-year-old son, Kris, in the car. We stopped on the way to school to buy a few groceries so I could give him something for his lunch. Mother Hubbard's cupboard was bare, because she was always at work. My son waited in the car in front of the store. (In those days, you could still do that without getting reported.)

Once inside the store, my body grabbed a basket and very efficiently and quickly filled it with the necessary items. My mind was already at work, preparing for my day. Yes, I looked very professional—all dressed up, high heels, and all—and boy, was I efficient! *There—done in no time. Am I good or what?* I quickly got back to my son in the car. My body opened the back door and started putting the groceries in the car one by one.

All of a sudden, I noticed myself slowing down. Something

was not right here. I could feel it. *But what? You know, I am very intuitive. Everybody says so. So I'd better pay attention.* Oh, my God! I hadn't paid for the groceries! No wonder I was putting them in the car one by one. There were way too many movements for one grocery bag. I quickly reversed the order, put everything back in the basket and raced back into the store.

At the checkout counter, the cashier's chin had dropped to her waist. She couldn't believe her eyes! She had been watching me the whole time. I quickly paid for my groceries, and we had a good laugh. For years afterwards, whenever I was standing in line to buy groceries, she'd share this story with the other customers.

I was not only time traveling, but also sleepwalking. My body did what it knew best while my mind was already at the office. The outcome could have gone very differently. I could have been arrested for shoplifting—not a very good thing when you're working in the prosecutor's office—and I could have been fired.

Now What?

WHEN YOU INTERPRET A CLUE, it's important to check inside and see if the interpretation resonates for you. If it doesn't feel quite right and you can't make sense of it, then just let it percolate for a while. Ask for more information. More clues will show up.

Beware of being solution-focused too early.

Let things percolate.

Give time for the answer to present itself.

My sister, Ingrid, had just finished upgrading her computer skills and was looking for employment. She had written down what kind of experience she was looking for—what kind of coworkers, the values of the company, etc. One day, as she was walking down the street, she happened to notice a white van with the word **Indigo** written on it. That's all it said. There was no indication of what type of service the word was related to. She thought to herself, *What kind of **marketing** is that? That doesn't tell you anything.*

A short while later Ingrid found herself reading an article in a newspaper about decorating. She rarely read the paper, but she was bored, and it happened to be sitting there. The article was about a woman who was using an **indigo** dress as part of her decorating scheme. The woman planned to use the dress to decorate the wall in her bedroom. Ingrid found the concept interesting. Both times, Ingrid noticed that she noticed.

A while later, Ingrid decided to visit her old boss at the art gallery where she had worked. Her boss naturally asked what kind of work Ingrid was looking for. On the spur of the moment, without much thought, Ingrid declared that she was interested in organizing. As they were discussing this, an old friend of the boss walked in, and the boss introduced Ingrid and said she was an organizer.

Later, Ingrid was visiting friends and decided to check her voice mail. There was a message from her ex-boss at the gallery. A friend of hers who she had run into at the grocery store was looking for an organized person who would do computer work. Would Ingrid be interested? Yes. Ingrid contacted the woman, and they arranged to meet. Ingrid was offered a three-week contract to work on a special project. Shortly after that time, she was offered full-time work.

Ingrid agonized over whether to take the position. I reminded her that the values of this company, the type of work, and the kind of coworkers and bosses all matched the order that she had put into the universe a few weeks previously through doing a written list of her ideal job description. She still wasn't certain. Well, guess what? The name of the company was **Indigo Marketing**! She found out a year later that the company hadn't planned to hire anyone for that position for another year, but they liked Ingrid so much that they didn't want to miss out on having her as an employee.

Take Inspired Action

CHAPTER 4

Take Inspired Action

What do I do with this information?
What is my next step?

S O YOU'VE SET YOUR INTENTION, asked the question or questions, and noticed and interpreted the clues. Now what? When do you act? When do you not act? All you ever have to do is take the next step. Taking the next step is manageable, doable, and doesn't tax you energetically or financially.

Let's suppose that you're looking for a new job. You've already done the work of asking for the clues to help you identify what it is that you really want. As you take these steps, the urge to take action gets stronger. But what action do you take? Again, you set an intention to receive information about what action to take to land this new job. You know what kind of job you'd like to experience next, but where?

One day, you notice an ad that intrigues you. It's in a magazine that you would normally never look at, but you're meeting a friend for lunch, and you're waiting in the reception area, flipping through this magazine. First, notice your reaction to the ad.

You're over the moon! This is exactly what you have been looking for, but you didn't even know where to begin looking. You send in your application right away. Notice your reaction. Yes. That feels good. Or something about the ad has piqued your interest, but you're still not quite sure. However, you're interested enough to seek out more information.

Again, there are several next-step options. You contact the HR department for more information and then compare what they give you to your ideal job description. It matches more than ninety percent! You apply. It feels good. Or you'd like to speak to people who have experienced working with this company, but you don't know anyone. You ask for help from Spirit. At a dinner party, you end up sitting next to someone who works for, has worked for, or knows people associated with this company. With each step that you took, you noticed how you felt, and this guided you to your next step.

Follow Your Urges

*T*HE URGE IS FASCINATING. IT is an impetus to take action. Urges take place on many levels: spiritual, emotional, mental, and physical. An urge is something that moves you in a new direction. An urge is a signal that a new direction wants to happen—a direction to what? You find out by taking the next step.

Of course, your day is not going to be made up of looking for clues all of the time. When is an urge not a clue? When it's part of your norm. A clue is not something out of the ordinary but something out of **your** ordinary.

As you are living your days from a place of what you want, then the feeling of needing or having to do something disappears. Because it is something that you want, then the action of moving forward toward what you want is enjoyable. It's a pleasure. It's a treat.

Is this a craving or an urge? An urge has an element of curiosity to it—maybe. Sometimes, an urge is so powerful that it's like the last few contractions just before birth—the big push. This is how I felt about moving to be by the ocean. I was afraid that I'd be on my death bed and would never have a chance to live by the ocean.

Initially, urges are subtle. If you notice them, you can follow the urge by taking small next steps. Looking back, I took many small steps. I was attracted to buying magazines on ocean living. I started visiting my sisters, who lived by the ocean, more often so that I could experience a bit of life near the ocean. I thought that this would be enough. But the urge just got stronger and stronger.

I felt like I was having a nervous breakdown. That led to the decision to sell our family home, get an apartment near the ocean, and keep an apartment in our hometown, a four-hour drive from the ocean. It took four years to land by the ocean. Could it have happened faster? Maybe—I don't know. Maybe my internal civil war about being selfish and uprooting my husband's entire life postponed my dream. We did end up by the ocean in a manner that honored both of us. And that I'm very happy about. As the urge gets stronger, you may need to take bigger steps or even a quantum leap.

What's the difference between a craving and an urge? A craving has a repetitive pattern to it that is temporarily satisfied when acted on but keeps coming back. Something wants to be expressed but never finds completion. Do the same thing with a craving that you do with an urge. Stop what you're doing, and give the craving a voice. Don't give it orders. Don't beat yourself up.

ASK, NOTICE, AND ACT

Following is a sample story which basically summarizes frequently asked questions about signs, signals, and clues. The story unfolds in a conversation between a coach and her client. It includes getting clear on what you want, asking for what you want, setting an intention, letting go, trusting, noticing your reactions, and taking inspired action through next steps.

SAMPLE STORY

"Amelia, what would you like to know about signs, signals, and clues?"

"I'm so confused. I don't know where to even start."

"Okay. Well, first stop what you're doing, and take a deep breath. And now another one. There. That's better. Now, what's your question?"

"What do you mean, what's my question?"

"Well, if you're feeling confused, you must have a question. What is it that you're confused about?"

"I can't decide whether to leave my job or not. I feel paralyzed by indecision."

"So, what would help you to make that decision?"

"A letter falling from the sky, telling me what to do."

"Yes, wouldn't we all like that? Let's say a letter did fall from the sky. What would it tell you to do?"

"It would let me know that everything was going to be okay, that I'm going to get a great job that I really like, and that pays me really well, and that it's going to be very easy for me to leave the job I have now. That there is someone who can take over this job who is perfect for it, and that it all works out for everyone."

"That's great, Amelia. What you've just done is set an intention. The nice thing about setting an intention is that it gets the ball rolling. You have now just sent your request out into the universe. You have just sent out a signal of what you want. Now you will be getting communication back. So your next step is to notice what comes your way. By that, I mean notice what you notice. Why are you noticing this and not that? Right now, when you think about getting a job you really like, close your eyes, and notice what sensations you feel in your body."

"I feel warm and cozy, relaxed, and my body feels bigger—not in size, but more powerful."

"Good. Now think about leaving the job you have now. What happens?"

"I can feel my throat and chest tightening. I feel like crying. I'm so worried about leaving my employer without help. He's been so good to me, and I've enjoyed working there—but not anymore."

"Good noticing. It's obvious that you really care for your employer, but now it sounds like you're suffering when you go to work. Can you imagine someone else doing this job—someone who would be perfect for the job and your employer?"

"I don't know. It's so hard in today's market to find people you can trust."

"What would it look like if someone showed up that you could trust?"

"Oh, that would be so amazing. I felt such relief when you said that."

"Well, Amelia. This is a good start. You don't have to make any decisions right now. What you can do is ask your guides to show you your next steps."

"I don't really know what you mean by that."

"Well, what you've just declared is that you'd like a new job, and you'd like someone to replace you in your old job who is trustworthy. You're not sure what you're looking for, so ask for signs that are clear and make sense to you to direct you to your new job. Meanwhile, have fun thinking about what your new work life would look like. What kind of people are you working with? What does your day look like? What are the parts of your life and your job right now that you'd like to keep? What are the parts that you'd like to see change? This will help you get clear on what you're looking for.

"Now let it go. Then as you go about your life, start noticing what you notice. Why did you notice this and not that? You'll know when something's information for you, because you'll have a reaction to it. You might feel delighted by what's come before you, or you might feel irritated. Just notice, and start collecting this information."

"But what if I don't notice anything? What if I don't get any clues?"

"Everyone gets clues. It's just a matter of getting in the habit and developing this muscle, just like any other skill. The important thing is to have fun with it. Be curious. *Isn't it interesting that I'm noticing this? I wonder what this is showing me.* Set the intention that you will notice the signs, signals, and clues. And then let it go."

"Well, I don't even know what to look for. What if I miss the signs?"

"Signs come to us in all kinds of ways. If you miss one, it will show up in another way. The important thing is to stay flexible. Don't expect the signs to show up in a certain way. You can't micro-manage the universe. As you become more attuned to noticing, your awareness will become more refined, and you'll notice clues more often."

"You can start by simply practicing using one of your five senses. This is just honing your noticing muscle. Set an intention to see, for example, four crows today. Another day, you might try setting the intention to hear the word *arbitrary* three times in one day. Or maybe you want to experience a certain smell. At other times, just practice noticing how many sounds you are actually hearing when you're out and about."

"Yes, but all that will take time. How do I get answers right now?"

"Answers come to you—usually when you're not focused on getting an answer. Studies have shown that inspiration comes when you're relaxed: when you're in the shower, or out for a walk, or listening to music. So ask your question, set your intention, and then let it go. Take care of what's in front of you. And as you do, you'll be led to the next step.

You may see a sign on a bus going by that clicks with you, or you may feel the urge to call someone all of a sudden, or to turn on the TV. And as you follow your urges, inspired actions are revealed to you. The next step is up to you. Will you take the action or not? Action steps are usually doable and incremental.

"Let's say you get the urge to call someone. But your self-doubt kicks in. *I don't want to bother them. What will I say? I don't even know why I'm calling.* So you talk yourself out of calling. But this same idea keeps popping up. So you make the call, and you say, *I don't even know why I'm calling but you kept popping into my mind all day*, and the other person says, *I'm so glad you called. You've been on mind all day, and I didn't have your phone number with me. I just heard about a job that I think would really suit you. You're probably not even looking for a job but I couldn't stop thinking about you.* And so you follow up. It may or may not be the right job for you. Maybe this action is connecting you to something even better. Do you see how it works?"

"I'm starting to. It doesn't seem that complicated."

"It's not. It's just another way of doing life—a more fun way."

"Well, why not—what have I got to lose?"

"Go for it!"

Chapter 5

Messages

A SIGN, SIGNAL, OR CLUE IS an indication that there is a message for you. What is the message about? How do you know when it's a sign? Why does this sign get your attention and not that one? Why are you noticing this and not that?

You will know when something's meant as a message for you because you will have a reaction to it. It either feels good or it doesn't. If it isn't a clue, you'll just feel neutral but more than likely you wouldn't even notice the clue.

The reaction may be positive or negative but your reaction is what has linked you to the sign. Your reaction may be one of delight at something that has appeared unexpectedly in your day. It will feel good to you. Or you may feel the energy in your body expanding or your heart opening up. Your reaction to another clue may be totally different. You may find that your reaction is negative—that you feel angry, sad, or confused. Or you may just notice a sensation in your body that doesn't feel good, like your energy has been drained. You may feel yourself shrinking or contracting. Neither reaction is good or bad. Both reactions are just information.

At the time that you notice a sign, you may not know what the sign is related to. Why might you notice something?

* It's a message to take action.

* It's a warning.

* It's something you might need in a few minutes or later that day.

* It's showing you an easier way.

* It's answering a question you may have asked.

Now what? What do you do with this information? Sometimes, the signs, signals, or clues will direct you to your next action step. Sometimes they fill in the pieces of the puzzle, one piece at a time, and you may have to wait until you collect more pieces. As you accept the signs as they appear—without trying to manipulate the information, just collecting the information—you will notice that you start receiving inspiration toward your next steps.

What's the difference between a sign, a signal, and a clue? What do they look like?

1. A sign is static, like a stop sign. Signs tell you the action to take and are more obvious.

2. A signal has movement—an element of activity to it—

like a turn signal on a car or over hearing a conversation. Signals have to do with timing.

3. Clues are static, more subtle, and are usually part of a group of dots that require connecting. Clues show you the path.

Let me show you what I mean. While I was driving the other day, I noticed that the car in front of me was signaling that he was turning right. We were all stopped at a sign—a red light. Everyone driving knows what this sign means. How did I know that the car in front of me was turning right? The little orange light at the right-hand back side of his car was blinking. It was signaling me, letting me know what direction the driver intended to take. How did I know that that's what the signal meant? I knew because I had studied the language of the road.

At some point, I inched slowly behind a long line of cars. I couldn't see any signs saying what was happening, and I couldn't see anyone signaling any information that let me know what was going on. But the fact that the traffic was moving very slowly was a clue that something was not the way it would normally be. At that point on the road, the traffic usually ran smoothly.

Now that I was aware of this clue, I felt the need to make a decision. Since there were no external signs or signals, I went inside to check my own radar. My inkling was to take the next exit out of the traffic and take a different route home. I could also have had the inkling to sit in traffic—that it wouldn't take that long—or I could have made a U-turn.

Signs, signals, and clues are the language of the soul, your higher self, and the universe. You will always receive signs in a form that is meaningful to you. If you are English, you will not be sent a message in Japanese and vice versa. Whatever has meaning and value to you is the language you will understand.

We see what we expect to see. What we perceive is filtered through the lens of our feelings, thoughts, and experience. So signs, signals, and clues are unique to you and your perspective. Just as in the dream state, several people could be sent identical dreams; yet the dream would mean something different to each receiver.

Just for fun, ask your friends, "What comes to mind when you think of a maple tree?"

Your first friend, Anna, may say, "A maple tree to me means freedom. It means Canada. I have freedom here that I would never have had in my own country."

Your second friend, Peter, may say, "I can't stand maple trees. Every time spring came, our house would be covered in maple bugs."

Your third friend, Luc, may say, "When I think of maple trees, I think of hard work. Every spring, we had to be outside in the slush and snow for hours, attending to hundreds of trees to collect the maple syrup."

Do you see how one symbol has different meanings for different people?

Messages from Spirit start off being subtle and gentle. If the messages are not heard or recognized, or if they're ignored, then they get louder. When is a message not a message from Spirit? Messages will never tell you that you **have** to do something. They are suggestions, and because of free will, it is up to you what you do with the message.

Many years ago, I received a series of signs, signals, and

clues that moved me in an entirely new career direction. I had prayed and asked for guidance in getting some direction about a career path. I didn't have a clue. I had just finished a nine-month contract working as an administrative assistant at a counseling centre. I had been a stay-at-home mom for nine years, and this work contract was sponsored by the government to help moms reenter the workforce. What was next?

Shortly after I finished that position, the board of directors at the counseling centre revised the job descriptions, and the **executive director's** position became half-time. Three different people asked me at various times if I was going to apply for the position. I was shocked. "Oh, no," I said. "You have to be a ballbuster to do that kind of job. I didn't have it in me." I started to feel a bit scared. One person was a fluke, but three? What did Spirit have in mind for me? I really didn't want to pay attention, but deep down, I knew something was going on beyond my own knowing.

During that time, I happened to be in the book section of a grocery store, and a book caught my attention. It was hard to miss. It was just about falling off the shelf. It was called *Feel the Fear and Do It Anyway*—interesting title. So I opened the book, and it opened to the story of a young woman who had just completed her master's in psychology. Her friend suggested that she apply for a position as **executive director** of a floating hospital that served those who couldn't afford medical care. Currently her friend had the position, and she was leaving. Her response was that there was no way she could do the job; she wasn't qualified. Sound familiar? *Oh, no! Another clue! Okay, Spirit; I will give applying for this job some thought but that's as far I'm going with it.* So I bought the book and read it.

A while later I had a dream. In the dream, I was looking for a restroom. (Whenever I'm going through a significant change, I seem to have toilet dreams.) I was in an old school, and I found the girls' restroom. There were no stalls available. Either the toilets weren't working or the doors were hanging off. I went back into the hallway, feeling quite desperate.

At the far end of the hall, I saw two men coming toward me. As they approached me, one of them spoke to me. He looked important. He was tall and handsome and dressed in a tuxedo. He turned to his assistant, who was also dressed in a tuxedo, and told him to give me the key to the **executive** restroom. Can you believe it? Now I knew I had to listen. There were just too many clues. I could have chosen to ignore these clues, but with great reluctance, I submitted my application on the very last day at the very last minute.

While going through the agony of deciding whether to follow the guidance I received, I experienced a lot of pain in both my legs. I knew my resistance to moving forward was showing up—another sign. It seems that whenever I have leg or foot problems, it's a sure sign that I am going through a shift of some sort, and it's time for me to change directions (which is what our feet and legs do for us in life).

So I said to Spirit, *There, I did my part*, and I let it go. I just knew I wouldn't get the job. But I also knew that by taking these steps, the door to something would be opened. Imagine my surprise when I did get the job, and a whole new career path opened up for me that I would never have considered. (By the way, my leg pain disappeared as soon as I submitted my application.)

Chapter 6

Where Are the Clues?

FOR MANY OF YOU, LIFE has been a guessing game. *Maybe if I do that, then this will work. When that doesn't work, I'll try something else. If I'm lucky, I'll find the right formula for success. If not, then it's not my fault. At least I will have tried.* What if there was a way to know that you're on the right track?

Where are these signs? Where do they show up? Where would you look for them? They may show up in a dream, on a billboard, on a bus passing by, etc. As you can see from the following list, messages from Spirit can show up just about anywhere. Three people could experience the very same circumstances but have totally different reactions to them. One person may think the circumstance is great, another one may feel neutral, and yet another one may really suffer from it.

Anything and everything in the world has significance. You

will know that something is significant to you by what you're noticing and your reaction to what you're noticing. Nobody else knows your reason for being—but you do. What you notice shows you the way.

Messages can manifest as **external** or **internal** clues. **External clues** are things that you notice outside of yourself and can involve anything including:

* Your environment, such as your home, furniture, car, desk, etc.
* Your personal items, such as wallets, purses, clothing, jewellery, footwear, computer, etc.
* Your favorite colors, numbers, etc.
* Nature, such as animals, birds, insects, sea life, etc.
* The elements
* The media
* Sounds, such as words, music, conversations, lyrics

Internal clues are more subtle and may require more attention. They include things that you notice inside yourself, such as:

* Feelings
* Thoughts
* Bodily sensations
* Urges
* Dreams
* Body discomfort, pain, illness

Negative clues include things that appear to be a problem in your life but are actually a tool used by Spirit to move you in the direction of your life design.

*   Apparent flaws
*   Missed opportunities
*   Arguments
*   Illness
*   Accidents
*   Pain

Everything in life is a mirror or reflection of what is going on inside of you. Just as we can't see our own faces, we often can't see what's really going on within us. Take a look around. What is your environment telling you? Thomas Leonard, the founder of Coach University, was asked what the biggest thing that he had learned in his life was. His reply was, *Your environment never lies.* Your environment is always giving you feedback about what is going on inside your life.

Some examples of **external** clues and **negative** clues follow.

COLOR

I've noticed that whenever I'm headed toward a big change in my life, I start wearing the color red. I may have no red in my wardrobe, but I become attracted to buying it, and I can't get enough of it. Then once the change has happened, I usually settle back into my more routine colors. Red is considered the color of action. I might not know what the change is but it's exciting for me to see what's coming.

ENVIRONMENT

I was running my coaching practice from my home. I saw clients in our family room on the river, and I also had an office upstairs. My paperwork had piled up to an unmanageable state. I hired my sister to help me declutter and reorganize. We got rid of ten large garbage bags of paper. My office looked great! Now it would be easy to take care of—you would think!

But within five months, my office was back in the same state. I realized that my **mess** may have had a **mess**-age for me. Maybe I didn't need a home office anymore. Maybe it was time to get an office in town. It turns out that that's exactly what needed to happen. I didn't have a clue how to go about finding an office space. What I did know was that I wanted a small, quiet, well-maintained, well-built office downtown within a certain price range that would be more convenient for my clients.

One day, as I was lying on a massage table, receiving some craniosacral work and looking up at the ceiling, I got the urge to ask my craniosacral therapist if she knew of any offices that might be available for rent downtown. Well, wouldn't you know it—there was one available right next door! I made arrangements to have a look at it, and it was perfect!

I almost missed my opportunity. I had the urge to ask my therapist about this in three previous sessions, but my logical mind kicked in, and I talked myself out of asking. The floor that her office was on was small and only had four offices, and they all appeared occupied. Besides, my therapist was very serious about her work, and what would she know about office rentals, anyway? Had I accepted my assumptions, I would have missed out on this opportunity. The paper mess was no longer an issue.

ANIMALS/BIRDS

Being Unaware

One day, I was sharing a coaching session with a client in the family room of our home. The view from our window was of a river in a beautiful mountain valley. There was always wildlife to observe. On this particular day, my client was struggling with balancing her personal time with work and family. She loved her family and her clients and felt very torn over this dilemma. As we were talking, a beautiful blue heron landed on one of the posts of our dock. I had never seen a heron in this area before. It sat there for a while.

One of the traits of the heron is that it always seems to be alone. It hunts alone and spends a lot of time alone. Here was exactly the answer that my client needed. The message resonated with her. She felt like she'd been given permission from Spirit to have the alone time she craved. In reality, this allowed her to give herself permission to have the time alone, since Spirit doesn't give us permission. It guides us in giving ourselves permission to go for what we really want.

INSECTS

Another time, I was working with a client in my family room. We sat facing each other on the large sofa. We noticed a spider crossing the surface of the sofa between us. I moved it to a safer place. This happened two more times in the same session. Finally, we clued in and realized that it might have a message for my client—and sure enough, it did.

My client was deciding whether to transition from having been employed for over twenty-five years to self-employment—a huge shift for her. We looked up the possible message from spider in *The Medicine Cards* (Sams and Carson), and it confirmed that going into her own business was the right thing to do. The spider is about creation. This wasn't the only thing my client based her decision on, but it was another clue in a series of clues.

NEGATIVE CLUES

A client of mine was a very successful artist in a small town. She was a very gregarious person and enjoyed spending the day painting in her studio downtown. All were welcome to drop by and visit. This particular town had an active artists' community, and rumblings about the limited available rental space for artists began. My client was being challenged about why she was able to get the space she had when other artists didn't get the same opportunity. She brought this issue to the table with me. We could have worked on a communication strategy, but instead, I asked her what she really wanted in a studio. She got quite excited as she described her dream to me, and halfway through our conversation, she said, *I have to go!* And off she went.

Three hours later, she called back. She had found the ideal studio space that matched all of her requirements: lots of space for painting and offering classes, a five-minute walk from her home, a private restroom, etc. And now her old space was available to other artists. Doesn't Spirit just work in magical ways? My client knew what she wanted but didn't know how it was going to happen. Spirit created a little push out the door to move her in the direction of her desire, and it worked out for everyone concerned with no hard feelings. Beautiful!

Sometimes I've had clients with their own businesses come to me, wondering whether they should close their business down because of the signs they received. They tell me they're not enjoying their work as much anymore. Most of their clients or customers are great, but they currently have two or three clients from hell, and it's enough for them to say, *I've had it.* When you are saying, *I've had it!*, this is usually a sure sign that not only are you ready for change, but also open to change.

Most of the time, this scenario is an indication that it's time to up-level your client profile. You have outgrown your business and your clients, and it's just not feeding you anymore. Your shoes don't fit anymore. What can you do? You redefine your client profile. You think about what you really want and go for that. And then you ask for Spirit's assistance and let go. You'll find the clients that don't fit dropping away, and you'll find yourself attracting the clients that now fit you—and you fit them.

Everything in your world is a mirror—a reflection of your inner world. Animals can also give us information about what's going on. When an animal crosses your path, and it's out of your norm, what might it be telling you? What is the nature of this animal? How does it operate? How does it fight, hide, store food, and communicate? What is its behavior?

Whatever stands out for you is where the information lies. What is your reaction? What thoughts and feelings surface for you? Whatever struck you first about the animal is what will be most important.

Each insect will have its own unique qualities and characteristics. Pay attention to its most unusual characteristics. Insects will often appear when you're going through a change. Metamorphosis of some sort is usually part of their message. Usually we don't make changes unless we're feeling uncomfortable. Ask yourself, *What is bugging me?* or *Who am I bugging?*

Chapter 7

Your Toolbox

*E*ACH OF US HAS A built-in guidance system that measures and alerts us to our energy flow. On this journey, you have been provided with a box of tools to help you navigate and direct your energy in order to create and experience the life your soul has designed for you. The tools are your body, your mind, and your feelings. Spirit speaks to you through your body, thoughts, and feelings. These are the mechanisms whereby you receive your clues.

Your body is the container that takes in, holds, and releases the energy from your Spirit according to the directions it is given by your thoughts and feelings. Your mind is the tool that receives information from the universal stream of consciousness and your feelings let you know whether or not you are on track with your life design based on the thoughts you have chosen to focus on. Feelings always follow thought, are usually experienced as a sensation in your body, and are the link between your body and your mind.

Your Body

*I*SN'T YOUR BODY AMAZING? ONCE you get in the habit of listening to your body, you will find that it is one of the biggest clue-givers in your life. Your body never lies. Your body is one of your main tools for assessing where you're at. It will always tell you the truth. The mind can play tricks on you by justifying, defending, denying, or explaining away what it is observing, but the body is a true barometer of what is actually occurring in your life.

What I'm talking about here is your physical senses being a receiver for messages from Spirit. The five physical senses let us know where we are in any given moment in time and space. We feel the ground beneath our feet, feel the wind on our skin, taste the food and drink going into our bodies, smell what is around us, or hear what's coming toward us or moving away from us. Everyone is familiar with those senses.

I just love how my body talks to me! It didn't always. Actually, it did, but I wasn't listening. I blamed it for a lot of things. I felt like a victim of its evil ways. Your body is a wonderful tool for receiving messages. How do you know when you feel cold, hot, or just fine? Your body has a built-in thermostat that keeps your body regulated at 98.6 degrees Fahrenheit. If it needs help regulating this temperature, it asks for help by creating goose bumps and shivers when it's cold and sweat and flushing when it's hot. Simple. You respond by adding clothing or taking it off, turning up the heat or turning it down. Simple. You trust the message you're receiving, and you trust the action you take.

Why do you trust? Because each time you've done this, it's worked!

How do you know when your body needs to eliminate something? How do you know when your body needs to take something in? As a child, you were trained to interpret the signals your body was giving you, and then you took steps to respond to those signals accordingly—to eat when you're hungry, drink when you're thirsty, sleep when you're tired, etc.

As adults, many of us have learned to ignore these signals, resulting in a lack of trust between us and our bodies. We have gotten out of the habit of listening to what our bodies are telling us. I've heard many people say that their bodies are betraying them when they have health issues, when, in fact, we are the ones who have betrayed our bodies.

When energy is flowing through our bodies at a pace that matches who we are, we say that we are healthy. When the energy becomes blocked, we experience that energy as not feeling well—as ill health. By the time we experience blocked energy in our bodies, we have already missed the clues on the emotional and mental levels of our being. We have not been listening. This is partly because we have been trained not to listen to what our bodies are telling us. Rather than listening to our bodily signals, we override these signals by ignoring them with messages like: *I just need to get one more thing done before I go to bed (even though I'm exhausted already). I shouldn't be eating anything right now; it's not even close to dinner. What's the matter with me? I have no self-discipline. I can wait to go to the restroom. It's no big deal. I can wait. I can wait. I can wait.*

Get in the habit now of inviting your body to be in partnership with you as you learn to listen to the clues it is giving you. Build trust by listening to its signals: feed it when it's hungry (it may only need three almonds), give it a drink when it's thirsty, or lie down for a bit when it's tired (again, it may only need five minutes). Build trust as you start to notice the sensations in your body in reaction to what you are thinking.

When you're having trouble making a decision, step inside—your body, that is. Take a few deep breaths, and think about the various outcomes. With each outcome, notice what your body's reaction is. Does your body feel like it's expanding? Contracting? Or does it feel neutral?

This is one of the quickest ways to determine what steps to take next. Your body can't tell what's real from what's imagined. So each situation you picture is reacted to as if it were real. There is valuable information in this. If you feel expansion, this is a green light from your spirit; if it feels contracted, this is a red light. If it feels neutral, it's not an issue for you, you may not have enough information, or you may need to reword the question to supply more information to your system.

For example, imagine you've been invited to a social event. You don't feel excited about it (that's the first clue) but you know you *should* go. Close your eyes. Take a couple of deep breaths. Now imagine yourself getting dressed to go to the event. You feel neutral—not yet enough information. Continue. Imagine yourself getting in the car and driving to the event. What is going on in your body? As you get closer to being there, you can feel your body shrinking, contracting, and pulling itself in. Do you have your answer? Yes.

Now imagine that you've graciously declined the invitation. Imagine staying home, reading by the fire, cozied up under a quilt, enjoying your alone time, drinking hot chocolate or having a glass of wine. What's your body doing now? You can feel your body expanding. It feels very relaxed. Do you have your answer? Yes.

Now, what if you noticed no change in your body at all when you imagined these two scenarios? Maybe there's a third option that wants to be experienced. And maybe right now, you don't have enough information to make a decision. Ask your guides for more information, and then let it go. Get on with your day.

Recognize that the body and mind are one. There is no separation between what is happening in our minds and what is happening in our bodies. The mind uses the body only as a last resort to give us a message. Every part of your body has a purpose, and if something is out of alignment in your life, and you're not getting the message, one of the ways that the message might be trying to get through is through a certain part of your body. When you experience things in your body, notice what part of the body is affected. Ask yourself the following questions:

1. What purpose does the affected part of the body serve?

2. What are my inner feelings about what is happening to that part of my body?

3. Can I describe the sensations, and what is going on?

4. If that body part could speak, what would it tell me?

5. How does this purpose relate to what's going on in my life?

6. What was happening in my life around the time that I first experienced the symptoms?

Noticing Your Body

The body-mind is its own problem solver, with the wrong answers showing up as tension and the right answers showing up as vitality.

A few years ago, I had hurt my left foot skiing. I didn't fall, but I had somehow twisted my foot inside of my boot. I limped along for a while, and my foot wasn't improving. By now, it was spring, and I couldn't wear my normal shoes and sandals. I ended up buying a pair of, what I considered to be, ugly orthopedic sandals so that my foot would have support. Finally, my doctor agreed to have a scan done on my foot. The scan revealed a soft tissue injury. He suggested a cortisone shot and said there wasn't much that could be done—that it would eventually turn into arthritis and that I would be required to get cortisone shots on a regular basis. I was not going to do arthritis, so I declined the shots and pursued other avenues.

I went to see a friend of mine who was a medical intuitive. She said my foot issue was about changing directions in my career and that I needed to start my own business. I didn't have a clue what I could possibly do. However, my curiosity was piqued, so I started paying attention to the clues. I remembered that another friend had given me information about a new field called coaching. I looked up the information and decided to train to become a coach. I now knew what my business would be.

I started coaching right away. My foot problem disappeared without any further intervention. It's now been many years since that happened. That same discomfort in my foot has surfaced very briefly only a couple of times since then. Each time, I knew it was about a change in direction. As soon as I got the message, the problem disappeared.

Feelings

*A*REN'T FEELINGS MAGICAL? HOW DOES your system know which emotion to feel? How does it know when to be angry? Sad? Happy? Doesn't it feel good sometimes to just have a good cry? Enjoy your feelings! They're there for a reason. Feelings are our tool for survival. We experience a feeling based on what purpose it serves us in this moment. For example, we use fear to protect us from danger, anger to define our boundaries, and grief to deal with our losses. Pain and pleasure are signals that move us toward something or away from something. Feelings always follow thought, so our feelings are a reaction to our perception and interpretation of what is occurring.

When I was growing up, people didn't pay much attention to feelings. Being logical and having common sense were the order of the day. Feelings didn't have a purpose. They were meant to be hidden, an embarrassment, and a sign of a lack of self-control and childishness. But if that were the case, why did different people react differently to the same situations? What made one person angry and not someone else?

My father was a man who had no difficulty expressing any of his emotions—sometimes to the extreme. And he was a very smart man. I admired him very much. On the other hand, my mother, who I also cherished, and who was an intelligent woman, didn't express much emotion at all. I never really knew what she was thinking. Why did she act the way she did? Why were they so different? Which way was the right way? I had all kinds of emotions I didn't know what to do with. Now I know.

Feelings are neither good nor bad. They are a message. Your feelings are your internal radar that let you know when things are on or off track. To read your radar, you need to be aware. To be aware, you need to be present. You are the witness. *Isn't it interesting that I'm feeling this way? I wonder what I'm reacting to. I wonder what it's telling me.* Feelings are a brilliant feedback mechanism—a report card that lets you know how you're doing, where you're at, and what's working and not working for you.

Feelings Alerting You!

Our feelings also alert us to when we are disconnected from Spirit and when we are unplugged from Source energy. Our feelings are the signals that let us know whether our energetic tank is full or not; that let us know if we're still plugged in or if we've become disconnected. When we're unplugged, we misinterpret the clues. Remember, feelings are just a current of energy traveling through the body. Once that energy is received, the circuit is complete. It has served its purpose. It's done its job. Now there is flow again. When your emotions are flowing again, you'll feel joyful, free, and hopeful. The goal is to keep the information flowing.

What many of us do with this energy is stuff it, shove it down, ignore it, pretend it isn't there, pretend it didn't happen, minimize it, shove it under the carpet, deal with it sometime in the future, or dump it on someone else. This energy, which is just a message, is then stored away in our body, unread and unused. When a feeling seems out of proportion to what has just activated it, then you can be sure you've got a vault of that same energy inside of you, waiting to be released. And you do want to release it! But some of you are afraid that once you start releasing, it's a bottomless pit, and you'll never be done—and jeez, you just don't have time for this right now! When these feelings are denied, they become toxic in the body. Consider your 'bad' feelings as signposts that you've taken a detour from your life design. Then ask yourself:

* What message does this feeling have for me?
* Where in my body am I feeling it?
* What is it trying to tell me?
* What was I just thinking?
* What did I just see, hear, touch, or smell?

There must be a reason that this is coming up now and not yesterday or last week.

Keep breathing as you do this check-in.

Just notice what is surfacing. (There is no need to dig.)

Ask for help from your guides.

Set the intention to receive the help.

Acknowledging your feelings is a huge step toward creating flow in your life. When the feelings are allowed to flow and be complete, then your life flows.

During the morning check-in of an employability program for women who had been abused and who were re-entering the work force, one woman reported that she was feeling really bitchy that day. As the facilitator, I suggested that she be the best bitch she could be and feel as bitchy as she possibly could, which she did. We all laughed. It was a relief for all of us that she had been so honest. We didn't need to second-guess what was happening with her that day, and then we didn't take her mood personally, either.

By being honest with herself, this woman was able to revel in her bitchiness without taking it out on anyone else. This was very empowering for her. By allowing herself to fully accept who she was in that moment, she was showing love for herself regardless of the state she was in. This young woman had lost her entire life—children, family, home, and work—through drug addiction. She turned her life around by accepting who she experienced herself to be in any given moment and went on to reconnect with her family and have a thriving career in the trades. She was an inspiration to me, because she was so honest about herself and her life. She had nothing to lose. And she came back to life through her perseverance in journaling about and experiencing her feelings.

Some people label themselves and others based on their feelings. Some people may have labeled this woman as a bitch in that particular moment. We are not our feelings. She was *feeling* bitchy, not *being* bitchy. Had she not honored her feeling of bitchiness, it may have expressed as being bitchy.

What happens when we don't listen to the message our

feelings are sending us—when we don't allow ourselves to experience the emotion, stuff it down, or minimize it? We then see life through the filter of this unreleased energy. It's the difference between looking at the bottom of a stream that has free-running, clear, clean water and one that is muddy. When we are not listening, we experience what's called 'emotional deafness'.

In my work, when I met with people who had experienced trauma, I always asked them to bring a trusted person with them to the meeting, because 75 percent of what I said would most likely not be heard. And in preparing them for their court cases, I often had to repeat the same information about how the court process worked over and over, because they heard and saw through the filter of their trauma.

One young woman in her thirties who I worked with was the victim of childhood abuse. One morning, I went to meet with her just before her court case began, and I couldn't find her anywhere. I finally found her lying in a fetal position on the floor in the witness room with the lights off. She managed to make it through the first line of questioning in court, and then it was obvious to the court that she needed a break, so the court took a recess.

The young woman and I went to the women's restroom, and she was shaking all over (energy releasing). I asked her what she wanted to do. She said she wanted to scream at the top of her lungs. I told her to go for it—and she did. She could be heard throughout the entire floor. The sheriff came rushing into the restroom to see what was going on. I reassured him that everything was okay. She kept going. This scream had been trapped inside of her for many years, and now she was finally able to access this scream and give herself permission to let it be released. A different person got back up on the witness stand—a person with a clear perspective—and the rest of the trial went very well.

On the other hand, most of our days are made up of a succession of a more minor expression of feelings. We don't know what feeling will surface at any given time, but by noticing what does surface and paying attention, we get feedback about our next steps.

I had just finished a contract and was wondering what I would be doing next. I didn't have a clue, but I knew that the signs would show up—and over the period of a week, they did. One morning, I was in the reception area of my husband's office, and I ran into a young man I had sat on a committee with. He was there to sign some legal documents—not a place I would have normally seen him. I felt a very slight shift, like something clicked into place in my heart area. I took note even though I didn't really know what it meant at the time.

A couple of days later, I ran into my neighbor at a bank that I didn't usually go to. I had not seen her for quite a while. We caught up on each other's news, and again, I noticed that little click in the same area of my chest. *Hmmm,* I thought. *Interesting.* A couple of days later, I was delighted to run into my husband as I was walking down the street. He and his buddy were going to lunch, and he asked me to join them, so I did.

During lunch, I could hardly hear their conversation. Two women were having lunch at the table next to us, and I could barely hear myself think, because they were talking so loudly. I could feel myself reacting. I was getting more and more irritated. I looked over to see who they were. I didn't recognize the woman that I could see. Of course, I wanted to tell them to tone it down. Actually, to be perfectly honest, I wanted to scream, *Shut up!* Then I started noticing the actual words they were saying. They were talking business, and I recognized some of the acronyms and issues they were discussing. This was my field! *Maybe I should pay attention here.*

I went back to eating my lunch, and I looked up as the two women were leaving. Now I could see the other woman, and I recognized her. I had listened to her give a talk a few weeks before. She happened to work at the same place as the other two people I had connected with earlier in the week. Then I remembered that someone else from that agency had spoken to me six months ago and asked me to contact her when I completed the contract I was working on at the time. So I contacted her. The woman who ended up hiring me was the same woman whom I had overheard in the restaurant. She was an absolutely lovely person, and I loved working with her. Had I not waited to see what was actually trying to get my attention, the whole scenario could have backfired on me.

Thoughts

I LOVE THINKING. I LOVE PONDERING. I love my mind. The mind is a wonderful thing. It's a wonderful tool. Look around you. Imagine what it would be like not to have a mind. It would not be fun! And that's what the mind is for—imagining. Imagining is the first step in creating. Your imagination is one of the most important tools that you have. Your imagination is what gives direction to the energy flowing through you. You can tell if what you're imagining is in alignment with your life design, because it will feel good. You are here to use your thinking and your focus to create. What you are focused on is what your energy flows to. You might as well focus it on what you want. When your imagination doesn't feel good, we call it worry. The same tool used in different ways—it's your choice.

I often wonder why I am thinking about one thing and not another. Our thoughts flow to us through our right brain from the universal field of consciousness. The thoughts that land will be those that match what it is that I'm focused on. What I'm focused on will depend on what I've invited into my life. Over the years, I've learned to be more discerning about what I invite in. How do I invite things in? I invite things in by what I give my attention to. I don't watch the news anymore, because then that stream of consciousness would flow through my system, and I would move into worry, fear, anxiety—you name it. My feelings gave me feedback that this information was not in alignment with my energy stream. In fact, it was draining my energy—depleting my energy. That was my experience.

Now, there are other people out there who absolutely love the news. They're very interested in what's going on in the world, and they use it as an opportunity to send light and love to those who are experiencing challenges. Their feelings are giving them feedback that watching the news is in alignment with who they are at the time. Most people invite things into their lives by default, unconsciously, and then take on those thoughts as their own.

Social scientists have noticed that about 95 percent of our thoughts are the same as the day before. Isn't that interesting? It makes sense, since so much of our day is occupied with doing things that are repetitive. But 95 percent of my thoughts are not going to be the same as 95 percent of your thoughts. So, what channel or station are you tuned into? Does it feel good or not? What is it that you are focused on? If it doesn't feel good, then notice that fact. Remember, the information is always in your reaction.

Sometimes the reaction is about changing the channel, and sometimes it isn't. So when something doesn't feel good, notice what you were just thinking. There are basically two feelings: you either feel good or you don't. When you don't feel good, your feelings are signaling you that your thoughts are off course. What course? The course you planned for this lifetime. By becoming consciously aware of your thoughts and redirecting them, you give yourself the opportunity to get back on course.

What were you just thinking? Is this a new thought? How can we change our thoughts if we don't even know what they are? We can do this by looking around. We will always be attracted to noticing what is a mirror or reflection of what we're carrying inside. How do we know if it's a match? By our reaction. The information is always in our reaction.

Have you ever noticed that great ideas often come to you at the most unlikely times and in the most unlikely places? As soon as you wake up in the morning, in the shower, or while you're driving, you get an idea. That's because when the mind is relaxed, creativity flows. Other activities that might induce this flow are taking a walk, playing with your kids or your dog, meditating, or reading poetry or a good novel.

Our thoughts are what create and tell the stories of our lives. Our feelings are a physical response to these thoughts that let us know whether we are on track with the stories that we are creating. Our feelings are our guidance systems—our GPS—that let us know which direction to take next.

What becomes your story is created by the energy that you invite in. Notice what it is that you are inviting into your life. Are you inviting in things and people that will support you in fully expressing who you are, or are you letting anything and everything come through the door? What story are you telling? Your words are your wand. You create the story of your life from the thoughts you think and the words you speak.

My twin cousin, Maion, had an old-fashioned flowered sofa that she detested. Every time she looked at that piece of furniture, she told herself how much she didn't like it and that she couldn't wait to get rid of it. She was very attached to not liking this sofa. When she found out that her family would be moving to a small community in the far north and that a furnished home would be supplied to them, she was absolutely thrilled to leave the sofa behind. Imagine her shock when she opened the door to her new home, and there sat an identical sofa to the one she just left behind a thousand miles away.

Maion's husband saw the look on her face and quickly exited the house. He didn't want to once again be the victim of one of her rants about the horrible sofa. She was using repetitive thinking and worry to create the life she didn't want.

She was putting in the same order to the universe—over and over again—of what she didn't want. She was imprinting the universe with a picture of what she didn't want.

Worrying: The Path to Doom

Notice when a new thought pops into your mind. Pay attention. What's it about? Can't get that song out of your head? What does it remind you of? What are the lyrics? Someone's face or name keeps popping into your mind? Why?

I was looking for work. My husband and I had student loans and we were just getting started after finishing our degrees, so we needed the extra income. We had just moved clear across the country in the past year, didn't know many people, and had no family around. Our daughter was just six months old, and I didn't really want to work. There was not much call for lab technicians in our community. I was told I'd have to go back to school for two years to become a medical lab tech. I had no office skills and wasn't really qualified to do anything else. I was very shy and even making a phone call was difficult for me—but I had no choice. So I promised myself that I would make a call the next day at precisely 10:00 a.m. to the department of agriculture to see if the office had any work available.

I had applied there before, and when Michelle was three weeks old, a woman named Barb called me with an offer of a temporary position over the summer. I explained that I had just had a baby, so I wasn't available. She suggested I call back in the fall; they might have something then. So that's what I did. I called, and I asked for Barb. I waited. Barb came to the phone. She didn't remember me or having talked to me in the spring. However, someone had just handed in his resignation two minutes before. She left to speak to her boss, and an interview time was set up for me. When I went to the interview, I was told that they were looking for someone with a master's in science. The fellow who had resigned had his master's. I only had my bachelor's—too bad. We had a nice visit and that was that.

A week later, I got a call back, and I was told that I had been hired. They were apologetic, because they could only offer me work for six months. I was thrilled, because I only wanted a job for six months. I wanted to be home with my daughter. Once I started working there, I discovered that the person who I had spoken with in the spring was named Theresa, and she had gone back to school. Barb, her boss, and the fellow who had resigned were the only people working in their section. My boss thought a government employment agency had sent me. Synchronicities?

Where did I get the name Barb? Why did I decide to call at 10:00 a.m. on that particular day? Did I receive guidance from Spirit? I think so! I just put one foot in front of the other. Don't dismiss those little inklings that you get!

Go for It!

I want you to have fun looking for and using the signs, signals and clues that Spirit sends your way.

So, remember:

ASK
NOTICE
ACT

*   Ask for what you want. What desires are being expressed through you?
*   Notice what you notice! What guidance is being sent your way?
*   Act on the inspiration you've received through the signs, signals and clues coming your way!

Enjoy the adventure!

Appendix 1

Ten Traps that Lead to Misinterpreting the Signs

1. **Making Assumptions** It's important not to make assumptions or jump to conclusions too early in the game when sleuthing for clues. Get in the habit of not making assumptions. Always go back to wonderment.

2. **Needing to Be Right** Like assumptions, the need to be right will sabotage your ability to notice and interpret clues. Don't argue with the universe. Stay curious! If you end up coming from a place of **should, must,** or **have to,** or feel heaviness in your energy, then most likely, you are misinterpreting the clues.

3. **Micromanaging the Universe** It will backfire on you! If you are trying to control the outcome, then you will see clues where there really aren't any. For example, you cannot tell the universe to make sure someone gets fired so you can have their job!

4. **Being Impulsive** If you are impulsive by nature, watch

that you don't jump to conclusions before you collect all the facts and connect all the dots.

5. **Overanalyzing** Do you tend to make things more difficult than they need to be? Messages are simple, direct and often literal. Don't over-analyze.

6. **Making Judgments** Judgment is the glue that will keep you where you are in this moment, perpetuating the thing you don't want. Judgment is the glue that will keep you out of the flow of moving from moment to moment and keep you mired in your situation. I notice that my energy dips the minute I have a judgment about the activity I'm doing, especially if it's something I have deemed as boring. When I'm in judgment, I extend the experience of the task I'm doing. *Is this ever going to end? It feels like forever. How many more moments of my life will I waste doing this stupid chore?* See what I mean? However, I notice that when I treat each moment as gold—as important, as meaningful, as if each moment matters—then my energy easily flows from one task to the next. I don't feel overwhelmed, because I'm only engaged in doing what is right in front of me. Much to my surprise, my tasks happen easily and effortlessly. As I am fully embodied in this moment, I notice the signals and urges of what wants to unfold next. This now happens quite effortlessly because my energy is not blocked by the resistance I felt when I was in judgment.

7. **Catastrophizing** Making mountains out of molehills or assuming that the worst possible thing is going to happen before you even have all the facts is catastrophizing.

This is a wonderful use of the imagination and possibly a clue of creative genius that, when channelled, could be used to produce a work of art in some form.

8. **Either or Thinking**: Either this will happen or that will happen based on past experience. This type of thinking leaves no room for other creative options and possibilities.

9. **Lacking Trust**: When you second-guess the clues that you're receiving, you show a lack of trust. Your job is to stay open and curious and see where the clues take you. When you doubt the clues that you're getting, you close the door to the perception of your options. When in doubt, ask for more and clearer clues.

10. **Minimizing Your Experience** This is the opposite of catastrophizing. You minimize your experience when you tell yourself, *It's okay. I can handle it. I don't mind* and do not acknowledge how you really feel about what's happening. Like judgment, this practice will keep you in your old story longer than necessary, creating unnecessary suffering.

CPSIA information can be obtained at www.ICGtesting.com
Printed in the USA
BVOW041435310313

316866BV00001B/1/P